JOURNEY
TO THE
MOON

Joseph McHugh/Latif Harris

CELESTIAL ARTS
Millbrae, California

First Printing, June 1974
Library of Congress Card No.: 74-9757
ISBN: 0-912310-73-1
Made in the United States of America

JOURNEY TO THE MOON

The key is touched by many hands, as the universe rolls out a starry carpet. The lock on the door at the end is a riddle: "What is it that is always, and has no becoming; and what is always becoming, and never is?"

The lock can never be forced open. To
look beyond, one must possess a key, ". . . then
he will gaze upon the light of the moon, the
stars, and shining heaven." The key is a
symbol, an archetype or a fixed ideal which
we share as common ground.

As Jung so correctly proposed, "The symbol is the middle way, upon which the opposites unite towards a new movement, a watercourse that pours forth fertility after long drought." The creative spirit in conjunction with the laws of chance reveals the key in many forms, of which this work is one.

The engravings from Doré and the quotations from Plato form a synchronous event when combined. The selection of the engravings and the quotations were independent events from individual spirits. The combination of the two formed a third which we call *this work*, Journey to the Moon.

I

. . . then he will gaze upon the light
of the moon, the stars, and shining heaven.

II

Out of disorder He created order!

III

... and He made the Universe a circle
moving in a circle
able to communicate with itself
and needing nothing beyond.

IV

He resolved to have a moving image of eternity,
and He made this image revolve
according to number,
and He let this image be called time.

V

The earth was created a living creature
endowed with a soul, and intelligence
by the providence of God.

VI

Being free of jealousy,
He desired all things to be
as like himself as possible.

VII

. . . and He fashioned a body
to be the vehicle for the soul.

VIII

That which is created
is of necessity corporeal.

IX

He created the night and the day
to be the one most intelligent revolution.

X

Of design, the earth was created
to provide its own food
from its own waste,
and all that it did or suffered
was turned back on itself.

XI

The body of the earth was created by God,
and none but God may render it soluble.

XII

The Creator looked to the eternal
when He created the world so fair,
for He is the best of causes,
and the world the fairest of creations.

XIII

When the Creator observed His Creation
moving and alive, He rejoiced!

XIV

The Earth provided various fruits
which grew on plants not planted by man,
and they dwelt in the open garden
free of shame and suffering.

XV

We are plants of a heavenly,
not earthly growth!

XVI

. . . and the true order of going
or being led by others
to the things of love
is to begin from
the beauties of the earth.

XVII

Mankind was given love,
in which pleasure and pain
would be mixed.

XVIII

. . . and the love of the Body
is an incitement
which chains man to the earthly Pleasure.

XIX

Deprived of God's care and protection
they were left defenceless,
and were attacked by beasts . . .
the food which once grew unbidden, failed.

XX

After a space of time,
the stream of heaven,
like a pestilence,
came pouring down!

XXI

Uniformity is to rest,
As motion to lack of uniformity.

XXII

To know the origin of Wisdom
is beyond us,
but we must accept the words
of the old Masters
who were the offspring of the gods.

XXIII

The gifts alluded to in the old tradition
were given to mankind by the gods;
from Prometheus they received fire;
from others they were given the arts.

XXIV

Unless one comes to an understanding
concerning the nature of Change,
one will have many difficulties.

XXV

The living arise from the dead,
the dead from the living!

XXVI

All mankind was made to share
the unique faculty of sensation,
arising from the impressions
rising all around him.

XXVII

We should seek for the divine in all things,
insofar as our nature will permit,
and always keep an eye toward heaven
and the blessed life there.

XXVIII

One who gathers Karma during one's life
will be changed into a beast,
who resembles best one's nature,
and will not cease from his toils
and transformations
until that revolution is completed.

XXIX

The soul that is fascinated with bodily pleasure
believes that Truth exists in a bodily form,
and will be dragged down again
into the visible world.

XXX

Each pleasure, each pain is a nail
which fastens the soul to the body,
until it becomes like the body.

XXXI

One who passes uninitiated into the underworld
will be unable to rise from the mire,
but one whose soul is pure
will rise to dwell with the gods!

XXXII

If one is to be of pure knowledge,
one must leave the body behind . . .

XXXIII

. . . and converse with the pure
to experience the light within.

XXXIV

After liberation, when one is compelled
to look toward the light,
one will suffer terrible pains,
and be unable at first
to see the glowing realities.

XXXV

Only God has the power to make whole
that which is shattered,
and shatter that which once was whole!

XXXVI

Time and Heaven were created together
in order that having been created together
they might likewise be dissolved together.

XXXVII

It is through the words of poets
that God converses with mankind.

XXXVIII

. . . for there is a vast chain
of dancers and masters
suspended from the stone
which hangs down from the Muse.

XXXIX

The pure soul is free of Karma,
and filled with knowledge . . .
for the seeker of truth
is a student of death.

PLATO & DORÉ

Quotations from Plato matched with the incredible etchings of Gustave Doré, the vision of each taken out of its traditional and, at times, narrow context, philosophy and art defying the bounds of man's reckoning of time.

Plato was a mystic and poet as well as a philosopher; Doré is best known for his fantastically imaginative illustrations for Dante's *Divine Comedy*, Milton's *Paradise Lost*, and the Bible. Each sheds new light and understanding on the other in this rich and beautiful complement.

CELESTIAL ARTS
Millbrae, California

The critic insists on Doré's acceptance of the mystical
as a tangible and "If, . . . , he has to throw a sense
of mystery and enchantment. . . . , he makes every
mountain peak and sterile vale, . . . , every lake among
black rocks, with cold reflections of the alien sky, . . . ,
every glimmer of the fading twilight, or weird
communion of the moonlight and the clouds, instinct
with marvel and with supernatural awe. . . ."

Gustave Doré was a French painter and graphic artist of the 19th century. He is best known for his fantastically imaginative illustrations for Dante's *Divine Comedy,* Milton's *Paradise Lost,* and the Bible.

A contemporary critic describes his work: "Among the special marvels of M. Doré's skill should be mentioned his extraordinary power of representing space. In many of his designs he seems to plunge you into infinity. . . . The sense of limitless extension is really prodigious: the eye is carried upward and onward, as if the heavens themselves were opening before its glance. . . . The doleful cliffs and valleys stretch outward into endless night; the sky oppresses you with its immeasurable dark."

The quotations in this work were taken from seven of Plato's dialogs. The translations, in most cases, are freely interpreted versions which do not lose the gist of their original meaning. As a poet and student of Plato for 15 years I kept my trust with him, not bending where the metal refused the fire, not taking away where the cornerstones lay.

The matching of the quotations with the incredible etchings of Doré was a simple matter. They blended well as the vision of each was universal when taken out of its traditional and, at times, narrow context. Philosophy and art commonly defy the bounds of man's reckoning time.

In Plato's central dialog, *The Timeaus,* he proposed a cosmogonic theory which included what we now think of as distinctly Eastern, as well as distinctly Western ideas. He spoke of one God as creator of the universe and a number of subordinate deities who in turn fashioned the sensible world and were responsible for the creation of humankind and their evolution. He spoke very clearly about the trans-migration of souls through animal and human levels, of the ideal Atlantis, and alchemical mathematics. He was a mystic and poet as well as a philosopher. Read in the light of the *Timeaus,* his other dialogs take on a new and richer meaning for our time. The mixture of Eastern and Western ideas has become an essential process for us today. Plato's location in time and place gave him roots in both the East and West, and the personae of his dialogs, as Greece herself, were bridges over which the traditional concepts of Eastern thought met those of the West.

PLATO & DORÉ

XLI

What is it that is always,
and has no becoming;
and what is always becoming,
and never is?

XL

He who has lived well
during his lifetime on earth,
shall return to dwell
in his native star.